DIGITAL DOLLARS

DIGITAL DOLLARS

Strategies for Success in the Online Marketplace

ELARA PHOENIX

QuantumQuill Press

CONTENTS

CHAPTER 1

Introduction

Almost all online marketplaces exist as a consequence of the economic principles of association and specialization. In a traditional open or mixed economy, individuals or manufacturers normally focus on a single good or service stream; this is where the concept of making things is important. Specialization is the other economic principle and it takes place in the real world when these teachers, painters, and other agents coalesce to form a society. Keynes condenses these principles into a single idea that captures the essence of creating value: "the division of labor". As human, personal, and economic learning and exchange continue in communities, different industries, markets, and methods of trade produce new goods and services. Some of these goods or services are intended for a local market, while others might be offered to the other side of the world at a later date.

Online shopping, or doing business or both over the web, is a natural progression of the web as a business delivery, shopping and commercial platform. A significant percentage of business research and commercial data indicate a rapidly growing number of online businesses and shops. New online services for young and old consumers are being offered on a weekly basis. Also, the general public has become more comfortable buying clothes, electronics, and other goods over the web. Finally, while traditional brick-and-mortar stores try to establish their presence and market space on the web, many well-known brands have reduced their investment in traditional storefronts and are focusing on the web. The web has exploded as a channel for getting and selling information and goods, representing five hundred million online businesses, ninety billion dollars in annual revenues, and at least one trillion dollars in available world market space.

CHAPTER 2

Understanding the Online Marketplace

The second major benefit of the online marketplace is cost effectiveness. It does not need large investment, and variable costs per transaction are low. Even small companies, producers, for instance, can expect to sell their items in the market. This study is a comprehensive review of various research on the concept, structure, and strategies for success in the online marketplace. The study begins with a description of what the online market is and what it is like. Then, a review of various related theoretical and empirical studies through different approaches, and summarized in a conclusion about research trends in online markets and potential challenges for both researchers and practitioners.

The traditional distribution channel model with one supplier, wholesalers, and retailers is now transformed into a new model called the online marketplace. This new model provides some unique advantages compared to traditional channel models. First, it provides clear information for buyers about various products more than wholesalers or retailers can provide. Buyers are able to get a lot of useful information about similar items at the same time, and therefore, they can make informed choices. This is the principal benefit of the online marketplace, and so it is increasingly used by traditional wholesalers or retailers, such as Walmart or Amazon, where each provides different similar items, but all are in one market.

CHAPTER 3

Building a Strong Online Presence

Once you have your website going, now it's time to update your store. You should give it a good design, rotate the merchandise that you offer regularly, and create promotions for your products. However, more than anything else, you must offer convenient payment methods. You want to persuade your visitors to go from visitor to customer as soon as possible and, in the world of e-commerce, that almost always means offering credit card payments.

Start with a great website that's not only full of useful content like company information, product data and prices, and contact information, but which also has a user-friendly web design. A good site is not just appealing to look at; it should also be easy to navigate, and content should be regularly updated. Open up a discussion with both existing customers and potential buyers. Social networking can be a great opportunity to network. Sites like Twitter and Facebook have a built-in audience of engaged users from all over the world. This is an easy way to gain attention from people who need exactly what you have to offer. Consider adding a blog to your website. Demonstrating that you're an expert in your particular field can help to attract new clients. If people view you as an important figure in your area of expertise, those people are more likely to trust what you say and more likely to become paying customers. Engage indirectly with potential clients by participating in message boards and forums. You'll come across as helpful and knowledgeable, and potential clients could get in touch after seeing your active participation and useful contributions. You can even participate in interviews. That's an opportunity for indirect brand promotion and a chance to inform potential clients about your business offerings.

Building a strong online presence does not take much, but it can make a huge impact on your e-commerce site. You can grow your business, increase sales, and save money on traditional advertising methods. It's a win-win situation. There are countless ways to optimize your online presence.

CHAPTER 4

Creating an Effective Digital Marketing Strategy

You begin the process of developing a digital marketing strategy by first developing a detailed understanding of the essence of the offer of the business, and then mapping the market growth, the space or specific market you are going to confront in terms of their growth characteristics, and the goals of the business, company, or corporation. You must also clearly understand that the market growth is a force that changes the market that you are confronting; that is, market growth creates new opportunities and it alters the nature of demand and competition.

At a high level, a corporation would be planning the following three stages to develop an effective digital marketing strategy - which systematically composes the three aforementioned issues.

There are three components of an effective digital marketing strategy: - A clearly defined Internet Corporate Strategy - A selection of one of the three most common generic Internet marketing strategies, i.e., What communication media you are going to employ to attract visitors to your Web site? - The type of communication you will have with your online customers, i.e., One-to-One communication or mass promotion

So, what are the elements of an effective (proactive) digital marketing strategy?

CHAPTER 5

Leveraging Social Media for Business Growth

A really great idea to take into consideration is a company blog. It is a great way to brand yourself and share what you do with others. A company blog can help convert traffic to your website. In fact, businesses that blog tend to have 55 percent more site visitors. Along with gaining more visitors, a blog can also help boost your SEO rankings. In terms of engagement, businesses with blogs receive a 97 percent increase in inbound links. Creating a compelling story will attract your current consumers, spread your message to new eyeballs, and could generate partnerships or even leads for your business.

It may seem overwhelming to know that there are over 200 social media platforms, and the number continues to rise. However, there is some great news: you don't need to use them all. More than likely, they won't all reach your target market. An example of this is as follows: a majority of Snapchat users are under the age of 24 and 71 percent of Snapchat users are under 34; this is a great marketing platform if you cater to users of this age. Some other social media platforms include: Facebook, Twitter, LinkedIn, Instagram, and Pinterest. It's nearly impossible to market to every single one of these. To be most effective, start with a few. Your strong point could be a different platform than another business.

CHAPTER 6

Optimizing Website Design and User Experience

If your company operates a company website and one of your interests is making sales or leads from it, then making the website well-designed is the best step to be taken, which you cannot forgo any moment. A well-designed website can make conversions, develop leads, amplify your SEO results, and elevate sales for businesses. Nonetheless, if your company is an e-commerce business, it is critical for the website to blow your visitors. So, in order for your company to cope productively as sales and leads from your website, the website must be fast, scalable, and promote online transactions. The following are the imperative web design categories to consider in each part of the website that your company owns.

The website's design is a critical element when it comes to user experience. It's especially important for businesses that want to make online sales, and the statistics emphasize this point. Just recently, a survey of online shopper behavior discovered that close to half (46%) of respondents believed that a website's design is their number one criterion for determining the credibility of an organization. 38% of respondents won't engage with an organization if its website didn't look good. 94% of the survey respondents contemplated website design an imperative element in their apprehensions about a website's credibility.

Additionally, 38% suggested they would leave a website once it goes unsightly. On top of that dismaying statistics, 48% of people reported the website's design as the top factor in their authority determination concerning a business.

As it is not practical for an online payment gateway to be able to directly engage with every customer and convince them to buy, the website's design and user experience must be an effective stand-in. A website's design and user experience must effectively and efficiently drive traffic to the location where the money transaction can be made. Websites that are easy to find, that promote and demonstrate their products well, and that have an effective transaction process can maximize the number of transactions that are completed once potential customers arrive.

CHAPTER 7

Implementing E-commerce Solutions

Consumer Financing As we saw in JCPenney's story, having fast online checkout options is important for converting sales. Walmart.com offers the Walmart Credit Card, Walmart MoneyCard, and a consumer credit plan. Keep in mind that, even with financing options, it's difficult to compete in many e-commerce markets without offering free shipping and a generous return policy. By partnering with strategic finance providers, you can offer affordable monthly payments and special offers to customers. Doing so can enable businesses to sell higher-ticket items to millennials who can't afford a 20% down payment or pay in full but who can afford monthly payments and special offers. This might compare to the retail market where in 2016, only 16% of millennials financed furniture, whereas 44% of Generation X and 40% of Baby Boomers financed auto loans in 2016. By attracting millennials to make sustainable purchases, businesses can build brand loyalty for years to come.

Marketplaces and Online Portals If traditional e-commerce stores aren't the right fit for your project, consider offering your products on various online marketplaces. These marketplaces have millions of customers actively searching for products. In addition to using online marketplaces, you can sell your products directly to companies, associations, groups, or clubs by setting up a portal. Online portals can provide the same convenient online shopping experience to external shoppers as they do for your existing customers. The Ariba Network is a sophisticated online portal that supports high-dollar transactions, such as municipal government purchases. In contrast, the WorkPlace Procurement site provides a simple portal for businesses that don't want to visit the main Home Depot site to search for the goods they need. No matter where you sell your products, be prepared to provide your buyers with the proof of sustainability they need to promote products to their customers.

CHAPTER 8

Enhancing Customer Service in the Digital Era

The digital transformation has begun to disrupt traditional customer service models, demanding huge changes in the way financial institutions have been advancing with customer support, usually subject to extensive and costly chains. The use of digital tools stands out as a differentiator in customer service and in promoting the improvement of administrative indicators, such as cost to maintain customer contacts, penetration, cross-selling, and customer acquisition. In this Digital Immersion context, the institutions together with their customers begin to dictate the speed, the depth, and the proportion of the changes that are tested and introduced on a daily basis. In the central scenario of Full Bank, as the central scenario of this article for the near future, both Assist and the bank, assisted by different digital channels, will present distinctive propositions and/or combine in all operations. Thus, they will have a growing number of products with specialized service (consumption of companies), from the distribution of a growing range of products by (individual) customers.

The digital era presents an unprecedented range of opportunities to strengthen the established role of customer service: creating customer service models that move from simple maintenance to a key differentiator in the face of competition. Develop unique offerings that are often the reason for clients to seek the bank's profile, including credit, ATM network availability, deposit promotions, and loyalty programs, among others. Customization strategies that aim to preserve the client and retain its operations within the bank have greater relevance in the client's asset products. Invest in the development of strategies to improve the earnings of the customer relationship. The evolution to a broad platform of services, not necessarily from financial institutions, allied to the best customer service – with the development of large self-service clusters, lean service approaches, named clients, and mobility at the disposal of the ample bank's product portfolio – tend to intensify the contact frequency of the VX client, allowing a better relationship with the client.

CHAPTER 9

Managing Online Payments and Security

Investments in developing mobile payment systems have recently picked up speed, driven by expectations of tapping into the fast-growing mobile market. However, selecting the appropriate mobile payment solutions has proven to be a complex task. Traditionally, one of the greatest challenges in creating a new payment system has been agreeing on and implementing standards. The problem is made more difficult in the case of mobile payment systems, where modern handsets operate on a number of different types of networks. Additionally, the level of security present in current mobile devices and their supporting networks measures matters of where, how, and by whom such mobile payments can be executed. Recent studies have situated mobile payment systems within the application/infrastructures domain, pointing out new directions in the architectural layout, design requirements, and the business models they might encompass.

Maintenance and patch management: If a vendor issues a patch to a digital process that you have purchased, it is important to install the patch in a timely manner to protect the digital process against newly discovered security vulnerabilities or viruses. As companies develop and implement contingency plans for responding to computer security breaches, the public policy debate about online privacy issues heats up. Government and industry are working on the development of data-protection standards for online privacy, including steps to further enhance software security and tools for Internet users and businesses to secure their sensitive data. Users of electronic marketplaces also should watch for news about data security and privacy.

Another major concern for new online businesses is managing security for digital dollars. In reality, the risks in conducting e-commerce comprise a subset of all potential business risks. Featuring guidelines for managing business risk, including the risks associated with conducting business online, the International Standards Organization is developing an extensive set of international standards. Small businesses should keep the three basic concepts of information security in mind: establish a policy for information security, manage risks, and implement and manage the systems in place. Moving to a digital process such as e-commerce introduces new issues.

CHAPTER 10

Maximizing Conversion Rates and Sales

You will probably find that the conversion journey for a particular product is not as simple as we may like it to be. Several statistical studies have tried to evaluate the typical number of interactions required to convert a visitor into a customer. The value-sum effect of countless digital dollar campaigns around the world allows us to come up with a practical estimation on proper interaction numbers. We estimate that it takes ten useful interactions with a potential customer to convert them to a 1st sale on an internal information search and four to six interactions for customers on an external information search. Providing meaningful and useful transition from each interaction to the subsequent one on the customer's journey to purchase is the key role of this strategic digitization model. Our research has shown that the majority of the useful interactions required to convert a first-time buyer are carried out offline. Remember that even customers that complete the Internet search process may never return to the website and opt to buy a product in a traditional high street retailer. Understanding how your traffic interacts with your online sales funnel enables you to increase the number of interactions by leading a potential customer back to your website. Your website information tells them to visit a local retailer who is actually stocking the item. Successful conversion of visitors to sales will depend upon how you work with your Internet and offline sales channels to optimize the dialogue with potential first-time buyers. The key process elements that must be understood and then thoughtfully manipulated to optimize conversion activities are based on providing the useful and meaningful information required from visitor to purchase.

1. Ensuring appropriate first interactions on the landing page. 2. Ensuring that the landing page carry-through is appropriate. 3. Ensuring that conversion is as simple as possible.

Of course, asking for the sale is the key objective of any direct response campaign. If the traffic isn't converted to sales, then all of the effort of attracting these individuals to your landing pages is wasted. Companies often confuse the difficulty of quantifying the exact lifetime value of a customer as a reason for not setting aggressive and specific sales targets for their digital dollar campaigns. If you do not have any online sales data available to use as a benchmark, then use our projected e-commerce annual spend in your market as a starting point for setting a realistic sales goal. The most straightforward method of generating online sales is to lead your visitors directly to your core e-commerce system. Your search engine marketing dollars buy you pieces of real estate on the increasingly expensive search engine results pages. It is vital to try and maximize the return from these precious spaces. The banner ads, links, and text ads used to attract visitors to your site play a direct role in determining whether these visitors convert to profitable sales. This serves to illustrate that every element of your search engine strategy must be designed to maximize the conversion of every dollar investment into a sales return.

Analyzing Data and Making Data-Driven Decisions

What sells? How often are views resulting in sales? How does post frequency relate to the pickup and sale of items? When and why do sales drop? Which keywords or product descriptors given to book titles are transferring to sale results? This is just a sampling of the types of questions I ask myself when reviewing my analytics every few months. Knowing the answers helps refine my inventory sourcing, pricing, inventory selection, book condition standards, and more. When sales are low, I might increase the number of listings available on a platform, promote items on social media, and research for different types of products, authors, and items. Should such efforts yield success, I know I am leveraging the resources of my business most effectively, and I use this information to make a marketing plan or content for social media; then I analyze how successful those efforts were in the next analytics review.

When we last talked, I noted how data is critical to understanding the health and trends in your online business and making informed adjustments. This week you're getting homework - I want you to look at your business data. From e-commerce platforms like Shopify, eBay, or Etsy to bookselling marketplaces like Amazon and Barnes & Noble, each of these companies offers a variety of metrics, often called analytics, available to sellers. You might have to dig for this information, but it is invaluable. Calculate your monthly and annual gross sales after platform and payment processing fees; idiocentric expenses of goods, supplies, and services; platform subscription fees; and general expenses including internet and shipping services, payroll, taxes, and fees for services like asset management or insurance. Store this data in a way that you can access in the future, and memorize the basic formulas so you can quickly validate financial details in the future. More importantly, understand your e-commerce business's financial health, and have a basic understanding of what trends in which metrics tend to coincide with successful outcomes.

CHAPTER 12

Expanding Reach through Search Engine Optimization

The goal then is to get on Page 1 either in natural search rankings or in ad placements. With respect to natural search rankings, here are some reasons why being on Page 1 is important: it has been estimated that approximately 93% of clicks occur on Page 1 only. If you are selling products online, this reason makes sense. People who are after kitchen appliances most likely buy from within the first page. A second reason is a study by Dr. Jim Jansen from Penn State University. He found out that 30% of all commercial searches resulted in a sale.

Most business executives love the word "target." They like strategies that hone in on a narrow segment of customers that they believe will yield the most profit. Small businesses in particular, expect Search Engine Optimization (SEO) to work in this respect - to identify the customers that will buy from them. They also expect - in fact, I have heard executives say this - SEO customers to be different from their other customers. Unfortunately, SEO is not a targeting strategy; it is, in fact, a filtering strategy.

"Search Engine Optimization (SEO) is the process of improving the quality and volume of website traffic from search engines by means of organic search results for target keywords." The goal of your SEO campaigns is to improve where the link to your website (and web pages) appears in the results when potential customers perform a search for targeted keywords. Fundamentally, your site's ranking will depend on the nature and extent of your content, your website's material, structure of your content, page optimization, web link building as well as social media linking.

CHAPTER 13

Harnessing the Power of Influencer Marketing

A new group of tastemakers has emerged through social media, whom we call "influencers". These are the people whom we trust to inform our tastes and preferences. They range from macro-influencers with hundreds of thousands of followers to micro-influencers with only a few thousand followers, but all have the ability to provide the surrounding culture with something crucial: the organic, word-of-mouth-based buzz that comes from direct endorsement by trusted taste influencers.

Identify the right influencers by segmenting your audience and finding people who either lead or are highly engaged with that segment. Research the person, not just their audience, to verify relevance and authenticity with your brand. Build and nurture relationships with those influencers before you need their help. And when it comes to initiating a partnership, lean on the influencer's creativity.

Influencer marketing allows your brand to reach a highly targeted audience of potential customers in a more authentic way than traditional advertising. Rather than trying to communicate with your target customers directly, your brand becomes part of the conversation among the influencer and the influencer's audience. This way, your message is presented as part of the fabric of native content. People also trust content from influencers more than they trust mainstream ads, making influencer marketing an extremely powerful tool when done correctly.

CHAPTER 14

Nurturing Customer Relationships through Email Marketing

The Procedure: When you draw a blank, and have subject line block; follow the instructions. Pull out pen and paper. List unique speaking points for your job role. Show that your company is proud to be part of an important sector. Include your social network, and smart phone applications. People love it when you mention Facebook and Twitter. However, remember, the message must be measures to speak to the 95% majority of subscribers, not to single out one particular subscriber. Better yet, why not try A/B Testing to learn what we should say in an effective correspondence to the audience? For every five words used in the email message, two to three words are about, or relevant to the subscriber. After the private informal introduction, you may start the sales pitch, or disseminate information. Follow this procedure, and make it your day to day habit to build relationships and keep subscribers. Following the formula, "the money is in the list," no expense of detail is given in this kaleidoscope of clever cookery that converts the word of word-of-mouth dimensions in the Eco time; Or should I say, the Eco hen?

"The money is in the list." Of this we are sure, but what is in our email marketing messages that makes a list so valuable? Let's look at the facts without dilution, if the money is in the list, and "Email Content is King," then the pithy content we send should fill royal coffers quite positively. Our email messages, or lack thereof, are responsible for listless subscribers, as is our un-thought out email program development strategy. If it passes muster with the three buckets email marketing rule, and focuses on pithy, to the point, well aired, intelligent and valuable messages, with relevant content that provides the subscriber with a takeaway, we see less of ourselves file our email as spam, we develop a powerful case for keeping subscribers tuning in, and when we find our marketing program is at a plateau, and stagnated, a simple email message appears to rejuvenate it.

CHAPTER 15

Utilizing Content Marketing to Drive Engagement

Digital currency narratives have had a substantial impact within the digital landscape. Blockchain technologies and currencies grant stories detailing the rise and fall in value, technical prowess, and notorious black market usage, leading to everyday awareness of digital dollar entities. Awareness of digital currency topics as Telegram channels, public Discord servers, forums, and threads all thrive discussing how users interact or have interacted with these products, offering an ideal environment for a rich content marketing environment. The echo chamber of the currency industry has led to myths and rites of passage. Create User — who outright refuses to use PayPal as a payment processor. Visit a digital exchange and deposit fiat/withdraw digital dollars. Political intervention and central banking scrutiny often lead to price speculation and potential product adoption retraction. A majority of content generated is concerned with the consolidation of power, decision making or enforcement, or price activity. While a majority of content is dedicated to digital strategies, the sustenance of a holistic plan can deliver the humanizing or idea-realization narratives required to truly drive user engagement.

Content marketing remains one of the most important tactics a brand can utilize to drive consumer engagement. Published on an owned platform, promotional content encourages consumer participation. With great potential while establishing some of the lowest barriers of entry for brands to execute, creating and utilizing content marketing effectively is crucial for any company. Digital currency enterprises should always be aware of and vigilant in updating the fundamentals of their industry. Content marketing can be utilized in numerous ways to generate consumer attention, with creativity only being the limit to the potential tactics employed. Brands should aim to keep content that offers users value at the forefront of decision-making processes. One-off pieces of content can have vastly different impacts on consumer engagement when not considering the holistic content marketing strategy as a unified whole. With the base focus shifted toward a beneficial end for users of specific platforms or broader community interests, successful content marketing strategies are easier to devise.

CHAPTER 16

Staying Ahead of the Competition in the Online Marketplace

Many retailers are adopting Digital 2.0 strategy, helping them to become more granular in their understanding of new technologies' potential, refine their execution roadmaps, shorten time to value, and improve the return on investment. Tech-powered retailers can use new offerings to push a wider range of value-added services (store checkout scan and go options, product review opportunities in-store via digital mirrors, etc.) into the smartphone customer interface. Such software loop can continuously grow in power until the experience itself becomes a competitive advantage that is almost impossible to replicate. As for the social trends, the recent experience of Covid-19 confirmed the major trend of moving consumers from offline physical interactions to online digital paradigms. On the business side, we are entering a post-industrial phase, where companies and field specialists are seeking new business models as the key to distinguish themselves from the competition.

Staying ahead of the competition in the online marketplace will require digitizing every aspect of commerce, from customer experience to back-end supply chain. This chapter shares examples of how leading retailers, banks, and service companies are refashioning traditional business infrastructure to deliver outstanding customer experiences and stay ahead in the digital age. Much like vehicle manufacturers are becoming software-heavy companies, retailers and banks will have to invest in high-tier software architecture to offer superior digital experiences to their customers. Our research shows that retailers are approaching digital transformation with greater urgency than any other sector. Over the next decade, we expect the overwhelming majority (80-90 percent) of global retail and consumer product companies to digitize their key customer engagements with software-driven business models, as they strive to extend beyond traditional markets and experience a sea change in customer expectations.